SO-ATE-319

Robb, Michael
Flower watching with Alice
twood

HAY LIBRARY
WESTERN WYOMING COMMUNITY COLLEGE

Purchased with funds from the

Wyoming Community Foundation

McMurry Library Endowment.

"A PUBLIC LIBRARY IS THE NEVER FAILING

SPRING IN THE DESERT." ANDREW CARNEGIE

1910
1970

CARNEGIE LIBRARY

CASPER, WYOMING

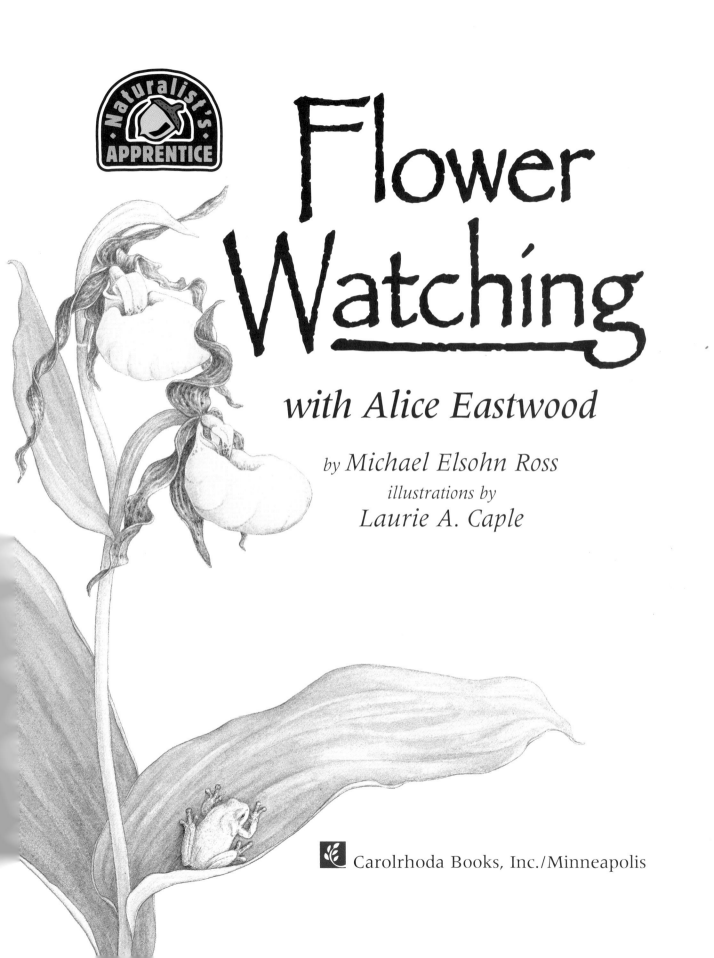

Flower Watching

with Alice Eastwood

by Michael Elsohn Ross

illustrations by
Laurie A. Caple

Carolrhoda Books, Inc./Minneapolis

In memory of my mentor, Dr. Carl W. Sharsmith—M. E. R.

For my son Stephen, whose reverence for nature is renewing—L. A. C.

Special thanks to Karren Elsbernd of the California Academy
of Sciences Archives

The illustrator wishes to thank Martha Benioff of the Save-the-Redwoods League

Text copyright © 1997 by Michael Elsohn Ross
Illustrations copyright © 1997 by Laurie A. Caple

All rights reserved. International copyright secured. No part of this book may be reproduced, stored in a retrieval
system, or transmitted in any form or by any means, electronic, mechanical, photocopying, recording, or otherwise,
without the prior written permission of Carolrhoda Books, Inc., except for the inclusion of brief quotations in an
acknowledged review.

Carolrhoda Books, Inc., c/o The Lerner Publishing Group
241 First Avenue North, Minneapolis, MN 55401 U.S.A.
www.lernerbooks.com

LIBRARY OF CONGRESS CATALOGING-IN-PUBLICATION DATA

Ross, Michael Elsohn
   Flower watching with Alice Eastwood / by Michael Elsohn Ross ; illustrated by Laurie A. Caple.
     p.   cm. - (Naturalist's apprentice)
   Includes bibliographical references (p.   ) and index.
   Summary: Discusses the life and work of botanist Alice Eastwood, who explored plant life in Colorado and
California in the late nineteenth and first half of the twentieth centuries.
   ISBN 1-57505-005-6
   1. Eastwood, Alice, 1859-1953—Juvenile literature. 2. Botanists—West (U.S.)—Biography—Juvenile literature.
3. Plants—Juvenile literature. 4. Botany—Study and teaching—Activity programs—Juvenile literature. [1.
Eastwood, Alice, 1859-1953. 2. Botanists. 3. Women—Biography. 4. Plants.] I. Caple, Laurie A., ill. II. Title. III.
Series: Ross, Michael Elsohn, Naturalist's apprentice.
QK31.E27R67 1997
581—dc20
                                                              96-27576

Manufactured in the United States of America
1 2 3 4 5 6 – JR – 02 01 00 99 98 97

FOXGLOVE

Contents

GOLDEN NORTH
BUMBLEBEE

4

APPLE BLOSSOM

Chapter 1
Alice in Wonderland

Have you ever peered into a poppy? Do you like to track bees through clover jungles or watch butterflies bopping from daisies to dandelions? Perhaps you have sniffed the perfume of backyard blossoms. But have you ever had a flower tickle your curiosity? Have you thought about exploring the lives of flowers? Scientists who study plants are called **botanists.** Can you picture yourself becoming a famous botanist, hot on the trail of flowery questions? Imagine a lifelong journey into the world of flowers.

Alice Eastwood was a famous botanist who started learning about flowers when she was a young girl. Over one hundred years ago, Alice explored the flowers in her uncle Helliwell's garden. Even though she was only six years old, he taught her to call wild raspberry *Rubus odoratus* and the red partridge berry *Mitchella repens*. She was learning to pronounce the scientific names of plants, just as you may have learned the scientific names of dinosaurs, such as *Tyrannosaurus rex*.

Alice's parents, Colin (left) and Eliza Eastwood (right)

Alice was born January 19, 1859, in Toronto, Canada, where her father, Colin Eastwood, worked at a hospital for people with mental illnesses. Mr. Eastwood had grown up in the woods near Toronto in the days when bears and other wild creatures roamed the countryside. He would tell Alice and her younger sister, Kate, stories of these pioneer times before they went to bed.

Alice's mother, Eliza Eastwood, grew up in Northern Ireland, and she had a sharp sense of humor. She had been in poor health for years, and shortly after Alice's sixth birthday, she became very ill. Mrs. Eastwood called young Alice to her bedside, kissed her, and asked her to look after four-year-old Kate and their baby brother, Sidney. Soon after this, Mrs. Eastwood died. Mr. Eastwood was so upset that he could not manage his job or the care of his children. Alice was sent to live with Uncle Helliwell, while Kate and Sidney went to other relatives.

For Alice, her uncle's home in the little town of Highland Creek, Ontario, was good medicine for sorrow. Her uncle's lush garden was full of birds, bugs, and flowers to investigate. Uncle Helliwell delighted in Alice's interest in nature, for he loved it too. Alice was on her way to becoming a **naturalist,** or a person who studies nature. She was also learning to read and write. Alice went to an early settler school with rough wooden benches and desks. She liked the other children and the books, and she soon became a champion speller.

After two years, Alice's father finally returned to care for his family. He opened a grocery store not far away in Whitby, where his brother, William Eastwood, was the town doctor. Being the oldest, eight-year-old Alice was expected to clean house, take care of her brother and sister, and go to school. She worked hard, but that didn't keep hard times away. In the fall of 1867, Mr. Eastwood gave up his store because it wasn't making enough money. He left Alice and Kate in the care of nuns at a Catholic convent in the nearby town of Oshawa and went off once again. Sidney was sent to live with a childless couple who lived near the convent, so the girls could visit him often.

The convent was a lovely place. Father Pugh, an elderly priest, had planted a large apple and cherry orchard. In the spring, the trees were covered with sweet-smelling blossoms that buzzed with bees. Alice and Kate played with paper dolls and a cardboard dollhouse under the lilac bushes. As Father Pugh tended the garden, Alice trailed along behind him.

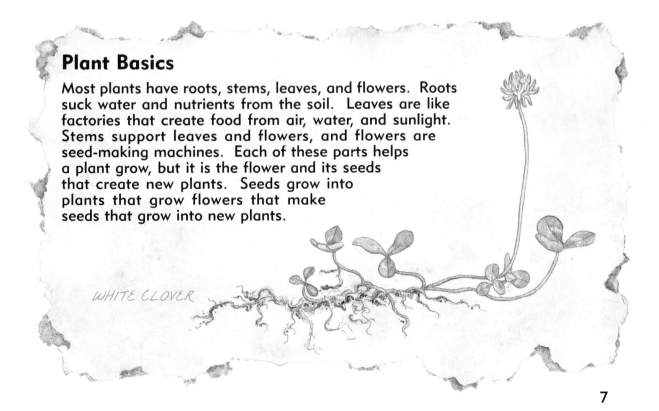

Plant Basics

Most plants have roots, stems, leaves, and flowers. Roots suck water and nutrients from the soil. Leaves are like factories that create food from air, water, and sunlight. Stems support leaves and flowers, and flowers are seed-making machines. Each of these parts helps a plant grow, but it is the flower and its seeds that create new plants. Seeds grow into plants that grow flowers that make seeds that grow into new plants.

WHITE CLOVER

The Catholic nuns at Oshawa lived a simple life devoted to prayer. Most of the time, Alice and Kate were the only children living at the convent. The meals were simple and the helpings were small. The girls' only treat was a spoonful of honey on their birthdays. For part of the time, the Eastwood girls were taught in a small school at the convent. They also attended a nearby Catholic school that was literally lousy—full of lice.

Since many of the children who came to the school had lice, Alice and Kate had to work hard to keep their hair free of the itchy little bugs. Alice also worked at learning most of her math by herself, for the nuns who taught had very little education themselves. Before long, Alice got used to teaching herself.

Once a year, the girls visited Uncle William in Whitby. Like Father Pugh, he experimented with growing different kinds of plants. Alice was impressed with his experiments and decided to try one of her own. She took seeds from geraniums, flowers growing in her uncle's garden, and carried them back to the convent. Could she produce new kinds of geraniums of different sizes and colors? In a secret garden, Alice planted the seeds and proudly watched them grow. Unfortunately it was autumn, and the frail plants soon froze in the

Plant Neighbors

You may know the human folks next door, but do you know your plant neighbors? Like Alice, you can get to know the odd and interesting plant citizens that reside in your community.

Go on an expedition. See how many kinds of plants you can discover. Look for blossoms and strange-looking leaves. Perhaps you can even find some seeds for planting, as Alice did.

Warning: It is against the law to pick flowers in most parks and nature preserves. Flowers are best left in their natural setting—where everyone can enjoy them. But before picking flowers even where it is legal (in your own yard, for example), be sure to get permission.

winter cold. But Uncle William had noticed Alice's interest and gave her a book about plants.

In 1873, when Alice was fourteen, she received a letter from her father. She had not seen him in six years. He was living in the Wild West town of Denver, at the foot of the Rocky Mountains. Mr. Eastwood had a job in this new city and wanted Alice to move there. Alice's brother, Sidney, had joined their father earlier, and now it was Alice's turn. Kate was to stay at the convent until her father sent for her. Alice was sad to leave her sister behind.

Upon Alice's arrival in Denver, she discovered an untidy town with muddy streets and saloons full of miners fresh from the hills. The shabby lodging where her father and brother boarded was also home to rough, ill-mannered miners and was not considered a proper place for a young woman. Mr. Eastwood arranged for Alice to live with a successful cattleman, Mr. Scherrer, who needed someone to care for his two young children.

After the convent, the Scherrers' home was a real luxury. The food was plentiful and good, and the shelves were filled with books. Alice read whenever she had the chance. She even managed to squeeze in reading time while caring for the baby—as long as she rocked his buggy or fed him his bottle to keep him happy. The best part about living with the Scherrers was that they moved up into the Rocky Mountains in the summer. There Alice found lush meadows with waist-high flowers. She was enchanted by columbines, lilies, and other blossoms that were larger and more colorful than those she had seen in the East.

Oyster Plant (genus *Tragopogon*)

Tragopogon means "goat beard" in Greek. The oyster plant, or salsify, looks like a goat beard when it gets its fuzzy seeds. It belongs to the sunflower family. The 50 species of oyster plant are originally from Europe.

Habitat: moist places along roadsides, fence rows, and other places where plant life has been disturbed. Plants are 1-4 feet tall.

Flowers: what looks like one flower is really a densely packed group of small, flat, purple flowers.

Fruit: hard seeds attached to stalks that look like inside-out umbrellas. Many of these are connected to the flowerhead, which makes it look like a dandelion seed head.

That next fall Mr. Eastwood began building a store in a new section of Denver. It had living quarters in back, and when the building was finished, Alice moved in with her father and brother. Before leaving for classes each day, Alice cleaned house, carried water, did the family laundry, and prepared food. Each night after dinner, she stayed up late doing homework. Despite all the tiring work at home, Alice thrived at school. Soon she was at the top of her class.

Change came to the Eastwood household in 1875. Mr. Eastwood remarried. Alice's new stepmother, Lydia Eastwood, had been a teacher in St. Louis. Alice was used to running the house and was at first upset by the arrival of her stepmother. She felt better, though, when Kate was sent for and the family was together again. But life was still not easy. Once again, Mr. Eastwood's business failed, so he took a job as a custodian at the new high school. The Eastwoods lived in the school's basement. During her senior year, Alice had to wake at four o'clock every morning to tend the furnace, while her father and brother delivered newspapers. In the afternoons and all day on Saturdays, she worked at a department store to earn cash for her books and clothes. Reading was one of

Alice's few entertainments. She took a new book out of the school library every Friday and usually finished it over the weekend.

Alice graduated from high school in 1879 with the highest grades in her class. Like many other educated young women of her time, she decided to teach. Teaching was one of the few jobs open to women in the 1800s. Alice was offered a job at a country school in the small town of Kiowa, Colorado, and she accepted. Surrounded by fields and pastures, Alice Eastwood could now immerse herself in her true passion— flowers. One of her high school teachers, Miss Overton, had given her

Alice Eastwood as a schoolteacher in the early 1880s

two plant books, the *Flora of Colorado* and *Gray's Manual of Plants*. Alice eagerly studied these books and identified the flowers around her. Her excitement about nature caught on with her classes. Alice's young students were becoming junior naturalists. Instead of bringing their teacher apples, they brought her rocks, bugs, flowers, and rattlesnake rattles.

At Miss Overton's wedding, Alice was so excited about discovering the name of a flower they had tried to identify on one their walks that she rushed up to her former teacher right after the ceremony. Before she congratulated the newlyweds, Alice excitedly blurted out, "I've found the name. It's the common oyster plant! Gray lists that because it grows everywhere."

Choosing a Field Guide

In Alice's day, flower guidebooks were not only expensive and hard to come by, they were also difficult to use. Many plants were missing from the guides altogether because they had not yet been described by scientists. But you will probably be able to find all sorts of flower books in libraries and bookstores. Try to pick a guide that has the following features:

✔ **Illustrations vs. Photos**
Believe it or not, a drawing or painting usually shows more detail than a photo. Go for a book with illustrations.

✔ **The Whole Gang**
Find a book that includes all the species, or kinds, of flowers that grow in your region, not just the common ones. The more plants your field guide lists, the more likely it is that you'll be able to find information about the uncommon flowers you might bump into in your own backyard or neighborhood.

✔ **User-Friendly**
Choose a guide that is easy to use. If the pictures and descriptions are all on one page, you'll be better able to make a quick ID.

✔ **In the Pocket**
An encyclopedia of flowers might be jam-packed with information, but it's a heavy load to carry on expeditions. A guide that can slip into your back pocket or fit easily into a daypack is just right.

✔ **Get the Facts**
Check out the beginning of a field guide for basic tips on telling flowers apart. The first few times you go flower watching, simply flip through your field guide until you find a picture that matches each flower you see. Keep the book in a handy place where you can flip through it regularly. Soon you'll know where in the book to turn, and you'll be able to make lightning-quick identifications.

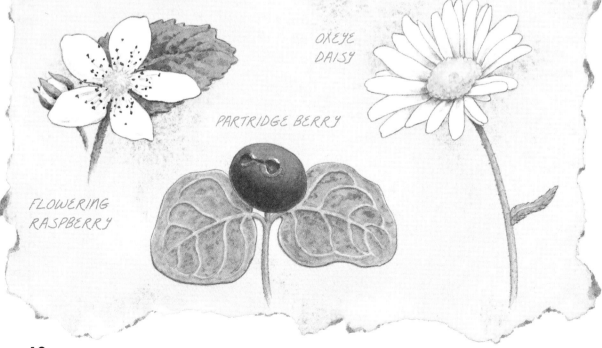

OXEYE DAISY

PARTRIDGE BERRY

FLOWERING RASPBERRY

Chapter 2
High Mountains, Low Flowers

During the summer following her second year of teaching, Alice Eastwood began to seriously explore the flowers of the Colorado Rocky Mountains. Alice had scrimped and saved her small teacher's salary throughout the school year so she could afford to travel and buy botany books. She was twenty-two years old and ready for adventures to out-of-the-way places, such as Colorado's Uncompahgre Canyon.

No roads led to the remote parts of the Rockies, so Alice traveled by horseback over the rugged trails. Women adventurers of the 1800s had to put up with a few obstacles to comfortable travel. Alice rode her horse sidesaddle, like other women of her time. Since women always wore long skirts or dresses—never pants—they couldn't sit with one leg on either side of the horse, as men did. Instead, they sat sideways with both legs hanging over one side. When women hiked, their long skirts dragged on the ground, and their bustles swayed to and fro. Bustles, which are frames or pads worn under skirts, made women look as if they had enormous bottoms. This getup was high fashion, but it made wilderness travel a real challenge. Alice dressed in a shorter, more practical skirt. It reached just to the tops of her high-top button shoes. Instead of the typical bustle, Alice wore her high-necked cotton nightgown under her skirt. Without the nightgown stored in her saddlebags, she had more room for plant books and other gear.

The Well-Equipped Flower Detective

Imagine yourself going on a wilderness expedition in fancy but totally awkward clothes. Luckily, people can dress in comfort these days when they go exploring. To be a well-equipped flower detective, gather some of the items below.

sun hat

magnifying lens

daypack with notebook, field guide, water bottle, snacks, and sunblock

comfortable shoes

Every summer during the 1880s, Alice explored the Rockies. One of the first mountains she climbed was Grays Peak, a 14,270-foot peak forty miles from Denver. She rode up the mountain in the company of three men from the East Coast who had come to Colorado to climb the mountains. On the way back down, they were caught in a wild thunderstorm. Lightning struck all around them. Alice wasn't afraid, but her horse was petrified. Everyone was soaked in the downpour, so they stopped at a boardinghouse to dry off. While they were there, someone stole Alice's purse from her saddlebag. Luckily, she kept most of her cash in the money belt she wore around her waist. Although Alice was disappointed by the loss, she was happy that the thief hadn't taken the flowers she had collected for study.

Despite the storm and robbery during her Grays Peak trip, Alice was hooked on climbing mountains and exploring their flowery gardens. On Pikes Peak, south of Denver, she discovered mountainsides covered with lush alpine flowers. With dozens of snowy peaks in view, Alice peered closely at tiny flower parts as she classified primroses, Jacob's ladders, and mountain forget-me-nots. She found beauty both in the grand mountain vistas and in the close views of tiny blossoms. Alice preferred to journey alone, for solitary walks filled her with peace and happiness. But occasionally she joined up with other travelers on foot or horseback. Alice was becoming known for her adventures in all the small mining hamlets and even in Denver. David Moffat, a banker and railroad builder, gave her free railroad passes so she could travel all over in her search for flowers. In America's Wild West, independent women were not only tolerated but often admired.

Alice (fourth from right) on Pikes Peak

It was no great surprise, then, when the principal of Alice's school ushered Alfred Russel Wallace into her classroom one morning in May of 1887. Wallace was a famous English naturalist. He had spent four years roaming the jungles of the Amazon River Basin collecting beetles and butterflies, and eight years exploring the tropical forests and islands of East Asia. Wallace had suffered from fever and the bites of leeches and ten-inch scorpions. Now, at age sixty-four, he was in the United States on a lecture tour, and he wanted to see the flowers of the Rockies. He had heard about Alice Eastwood and asked her to guide him through the alpine gardens of Grays Peak.

Alice was thrilled by the request and gladly agreed to be Wallace's guide. She had read about his journeys and his scientific theories. They made their trip in July, when the mountain was a carpet of reds, blues, yellows, and pinks. One of the most spectacular flowers they saw was the showy columbine. They explored for several days, and on the last day, they climbed to the top of the peak.

Columbine (genus *Aquilegia*)

Member of the buttercup family, which also includes larkspurs, meadow rue, monkshood, and buttercups (of course). Over 65 species of columbine in the world. The Rocky Mountain columbine is the state flower of Colorado.

Habitat: most grow in moist places from sea level to the tops of mountains.

Flowers: 5 spur-like petals, 5 petal-like sepals, many stamens, and 5 pistils

Fruit: 5 dry, pointed pods with many small seeds

ROCKY MOUNTAIN COLUMBINE

How to Use a Magnifying Lens

Besides field guides, one of the handiest botanical tools is a magnifying lens. Alice always carried her prized Swiss lens. Many flower parts are clearly visible only through a five- or ten-power lens. A five-power (5X) lens makes things look five times bigger than they really are, and a ten-power (10X) lens makes things look ten times bigger. Lenses with less power are not very useful for exploring flowers.

✔ If you don't have a hand lens, borrow or buy one. Good 5X or 10X lenses are usually available for less than ten dollars.

✔ Hold the lens up in front of one eye and close the other. If you can't keep your eye closed by blinking, use your finger to hold the lid shut.

✔ Look at an object through the lens by moving toward what you are viewing until you can see it clearly. Lenses work best when they are held close to your eye.

✔ Now find some flowers in your backyard, garden, or local park. Check them out with your lens. Do you notice anything new?

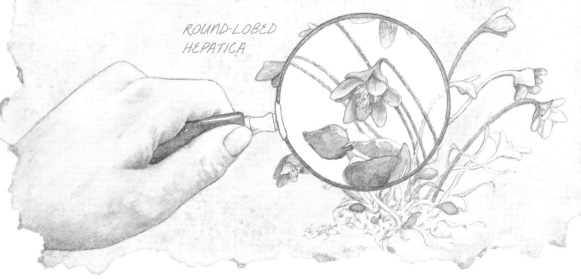

ROUND-LOBED HEPATICA

While Alice's legs helped her hike to the top of the loftiest mountains, her eyes helped her descend into the tiniest flowers. Here within the delicate blossoms, she discovered not only strange, exquisite beauty, but clues to the identity of each plant. Botanists pay very close attention to the parts of plants. They note the color, texture, and shape of leaves. They examine and describe the appearance of roots. Even the tiny structures hidden within a flower are peered at seriously. Through a magnifying lens, the inside of a flower may look like an ant's playground or a Martian's house, but it's really a place where seeds are made.

Climbing into Flowers

As you probably know, most flowers have brightly colored **petals.** But are you aware that there are male and female parts inside the blossoms? The male parts of flowers are called **stamens.** These contain **pollen,** which is needed for making seeds. The female parts are called the **pistils.** Inside the pistils are eggs. Underneath the petals are leaflike parts called **sepals.** The last time you ate a strawberry, you probably picked off the sepals before popping the berry into your mouth. Most flowers that you run across will have all these parts, but some species may lack one part or another.

When pollen comes in contact with the eggs, seeds form inside the pistil, which gradually grows into a fruit. Fruits can be fleshy or dry and can contain one or more seeds.

Take a journey into some local blossoms and see flower parts for yourself. How many petals can you find? What color and shape are they? How many stamens and pistils can you count? What shape are they? Can you see any of the green sepals underneath the petals? Look at the ends of the stamens. Do you see powdery stuff? That's pollen.

WILD OR COMMON STRAWBERRY

Alice continued to teach during the school year and to save her salary for books and summer trips. She even had enough extra money to buy some downtown property in Denver with her father. Each year as soon as the school term was over, Alice was ready for botanical journeys to the peaks and high deserts of the Rocky Mountain region. On every one of these trips, Alice collected plants. During the 1800s, scientists on the East Coast and in Europe had been collecting, comparing, and naming plants from all over the world. But they knew very little about what kinds of plants grew in the western United States. They were eager to find out. Even

Alice used a plant press to preserve the plants she found on her travels.

though Alice was a self-taught rather than professionally trained botanist, her knowledge of western plants made her an important part of this international network of scientists.

For Alice, each plant she found was a treasure. Botanists like Alice needed to collect plants so they could study them at home to determine their identity. With care, she would dig a plant from the earth, roots and all, and place it in her plant press. A plant press is like a suitcase for plants. Plants are carefully laid on sheets of paper, which are then sandwiched between two wooden frames. The press is bound tightly with straps, and the plants are flattened and protected. Alice had to air her specimens out by the campfire each night to keep them from molding. In her notebooks, she recorded where each plant had been found. Alice later discovered that some plants were so rare, it was only through her notes that other botanists were able to find the way to their hidden gardens.

Alice carried very little in her saddlebag other than her plant books and collections. Her meals, like those at the convent, were very simple. Sometimes all she ate was bread. As she explored out-of-the-way canyons and **mesas,** Alice identified as many plants as she could, using the books she carried in her saddlebag. These books had few pictures, because pictures would have made the books too expensive and bulky. Instead, the guides came with an ingenious tool called a key—a key to unlocking the identities of plants.

On Key

Are you ready to try a plant key like the kind Alice used? Below are pictures of four common yellow flowers. Let's imagine they all grow in the same park. Choose one of the flowers shown and pretend it's a flower that you discovered on a walk. You want to know its name. As you examine the picture of the flower, read through the key. The key will ask you questions. Answer as best as you can and go where the key tells you. If you are confused by some of the terms for plant parts, you may want to check out the diagram on page 18. Good luck! (To check your answers, see page 45.)

Key to Yellow Flowers

Are there 5 petals? If yes, go to ✳. If no, go to ❀.

✳ Are the petals notched at the end? If yes, you have *Potentilla recta* (rough-fruited cinquefoil). If no, go to ◖.

  ◖ Are the petal edges wavy but not notched? If yes, you have *Ranunculus bulbosus* (bulbous buttercup). If no, start over and try again.

❀ Are there 4 petals? If yes, go to ⚜. If no, start again.

  ⚜ Are there 8 stamens? If yes, you have *Oenothera biennis* (evening primrose). If no, go to ⚜.

  ⚜ Are there 6 stamens? If yes, you have *Brassica rapa* (field mustard). If no, start over and try again.

How did it work? If you were able to find the names of these four flowers using this key, you may be ready to use the key in a regional flower guide to unlock the names of hundreds of flowers.

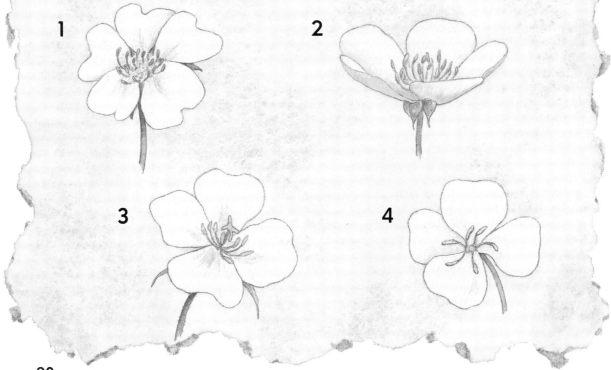

CALIFORNIA POPPY

Chapter 3
California Adventures

By 1890, Denver had grown into a real city. The downtown property that Alice and her father owned had become very valuable. When they sold it, Alice earned ten thousand dollars, which was a lot of money at that time—her teaching salary was only one hundred dollars a month. Alice decided to quit teaching and build a couple of rental houses in the new mining town of Durango, Colorado. With rent from these houses, she could afford to retire. Thirty-one-year-old Alice was ready to devote her life to botanical adventures!

Toward the end of December 1890, Alice boarded a train for California. Near San Diego, she was excited to discover the unique plants of the southern California mesas and coasts. Some of these plants, such as the California poppy, which carpeted the hillsides in the spring, were unlike any flowers she had seen in the Rockies. During the day, Alice searched for plants, often carrying only a bag of olives for lunch. She was retired but not rich, and she had to be careful with her money. At night or on rainy days, Alice examined her plant specimens and looked them up in her books.

Alice was excited to meet Katharine and Townshend Brandegee (above) at the California Academy of Sciences (left) in downtown San Francisco.

In May, Alice traveled up the coast, collecting all the way. She saw her first redwoods, the world's tallest trees, as well as many other wonderful plants, in Santa Cruz. Finally, she arrived in San Francisco, a new and beautiful city. But Alice hadn't come to San Francisco as a tourist—it was home to the California Academy of Sciences, the largest scientific organization in the West. This group had been started forty years before by well-known naturalists. The academy had built a magnificent six-story building in downtown San Francisco to house its natural history collections and offices. Marble stairs led up from an open entry hall lined with six levels of balcony-bordered rooms.

Alice was anxious to meet Katharine Brandegee and her husband, Townshend. Mrs. Brandegee was the curator—the person in charge—of the academy's **herbarium,** or plant collection. She was one of the few women naturalists in the country to have such a prestigious job. Mr. Brandegee had collected and given names to many species of plants while exploring the Rockies twenty years before. The Brandegees were also editors of a nature journal called *Zoe.* They were like heroes to Alice, for she wanted to study and write about plants just as they had.

Alice found the Brandegees on the sixth floor of the academy building, leaning over a large wooden table examining pressed, dried plants. The air smelled like mothballs because of the chemicals used to keep bugs from eating the plants. Rows of wooden cabinets filled with dried plants lined the walls. Some had been collected long before Alice was even born!

Under her arm, Alice carried folders of pressed plants from her California explorations. The Brandegees happily looked over her plant specimens and praised her careful work. They had heard of Alice's Colorado collections and of her trip up Grays Peak with Alfred Russel Wallace. They asked Alice to accompany them on a hike to look for plants.

Alice enjoyed California, but she returned to the Rockies anxious to explore more mountain gardens. Later in 1891, the Brandegees, who were on their way home from a trip to the East Coast, visited Alice in Denver. They were amazed by Alice's carefully organized plant collection, and Katharine asked Alice to be her assistant at the Academy of Sciences for the winter. Alice accepted and, before long, moved to San Francisco.

Alice worked hard, and the Brandegees were pleased with her work. They even helped her become a member of the Academy of Sciences. But Alice had no intention of abandoning her summer wanderings in the Rocky Mountains. In the spring of 1892, she explored the canyon country of southeastern Utah with friends. The desert was in full bloom. They rode past fields of sky-colored lupines and crimson asters.

Settled in Colorado once more, Alice completed a book about the flowers of Denver, which she published with her own money. And she met a young journalist from the East who had come to Denver to find a cure for his poor health. Alice fell in love with him and, for the first time, considered marriage. Then she received a letter from Katharine Brandegee offering her a position as joint curator of the collections. Alice was very interested. But she liked being in Denver. She was close to the Rockies, she was near her family, and she was in love. In the midst of trying to come to a decision, the health of her journalist worsened, and he soon died. Saddened by this loss, Alice decided to leave Denver. She wrote Katharine Brandegee to say that she would accept the job, and in December of 1892, Alice returned to San Francisco.

As joint curator of the herbarium, Alice took part in organizing the plants for the collection. But she also traveled all over California to search for plants. Alice's first official collecting trip for the herbarium was to the remote rangelands of the southern San Joaquin Valley in the spring of 1893. There Alice found prairies lush with wildflowers, watered by mountain streams.

DESERT
COTTONTAIL
RABBIT

PRAIRIE WILDFLOWERS

Unlike many other women of her time, Alice was not worried about exploring vast landscapes alone. During her hours of solitude, she was busy writing, collecting, and sketching. Since many plants were still unknown to scientists, Alice's main duty was to add to the academy's collections.

Botanical Journal

Botanists rarely find new plants any longer, so there is less need to collect plants. Plant collecting in most places is allowed only if you have a special collecting permit. But you can collect plants without picking them by drawing, photographing, or writing about them. Like Alice, you can use a journal to record what they look like, where you find them, when they bloom, and other interesting information.

Supplies
✔ sketchbook or scrap paper
✔ clipboard or other hard writing and drawing surface
✔ pen or pencil
✔ colored pens or pencils
✔ magnifying lens
✔ camera (optional)

Trillium May 1st.

What to Do

✔ A good way to start sketching is to draw flower parts one by one rather than worrying about the whole flower. Make some quick sketches of the different parts you see. See if you can match some of the colors or draw some of the patterns that you notice. Sketching each part will prepare you for drawing the entire flower.

✔ When you feel ready to draw the outline of a whole flower, pretend your eyes are tiny bugs. Let them crawl up the stem, over the leaves and sepals, and onto the petals. Allow them to play around in the stamens and pistils. As your eyes travel, let your pencil record the path.

✔ Next to your drawing, write down the name of the flower (if you know it) and any other interesting information.

✔ If you have a camera, take a picture of the flower and attach a photo to your journal page.

✔ If a friend has similar plants growing near his or her house, compare the dates when flowers pop open or share observations about the bugs that visit your flowers.

Across the bay, north of San Francisco, loomed Mount Tamalpais. On Sundays, Alice would cross the bay by ferry, then catch a train to the base of the mountain. She would spend the day looking for plants. To get back in time for the last train, Alice sometimes had to hike at full speed. She spent so much time walking that she could hike at a pace of four miles an hour without tiring. While exploring every part of the mountain searching for new plants, Alice became an expert on the trails.

One weekend Alice was invited to join an all-male hiking club on an outing. The club was making a map of the Mount Tamalpais trails and needed her help. At first they intended to have Alice along for just one hike, but after she out-hiked many of the men, she was warmly initiated into the club. Being the only woman member of an all-male club didn't seem to bother her at all. Though Alice had plenty of male companions on wilderness treks, she didn't seem to care about getting married.

In August of 1893, Alice embarked on a collecting trip to Mount Shasta. This huge, extinct volcano in northern California is covered with snow even in the summer and is known for its unpredictable and sometimes deadly weather. Alice had little interest in hiking to the very top, because most of the plants were lower on the mountain. But a group of young men begged her to join them on their climb. Although she lacked necessary equipment, such as cleats in her shoes and sunglasses, and was wearing a heavy corduroy skirt, Alice accepted the invitation. They blackened their faces with charcoal to prevent sunburn and started hiking at 2 A.M. The freezing cold didn't stop Alice from collecting plants along the way. The hikers plunged through snow, carefully avoiding deep cracks, and eventually reached the summit. The way down went much faster. The men slid down on burlap sacks worn like diapers, and Alice used her skirt as a sled.

Even when she wasn't on an official expedition, Alice always had her eyes on plants. As she walked to work at the academy, she identified the plants that grew in the cracks of the cobblestone streets. To Alice, these plants were the hardiest of plant pioneers. Among the sixty-four species she once counted were plants from as far away as New Zealand, Africa, and South America. These plants had come to California with people from these far lands.

"The cobblestones afford protection to many a tiny plant even where traffic is considerable," wrote Alice in an article, "while on the hills that are too steep to permit anything except the cable cars being hauled up and down, a wilderness of plants appear, often so dense as to conceal the cobblestones beneath. It is refreshing among so much that is dirty, shabby, and ugly in the city streets . . . to reflect how nature tries to cover over the defacements of man and once again make all beautiful."

Few native California plants seemed to survive the wagon wheels and horse hooves. One that made its home in the sidewalk cracks was a tiny plant called pineapple weed—the flowerhead looks like a small pineapple. This native Californian thrives in trampled places and has spread across the United States. It is often considered a weed because it grows where it is not wanted.

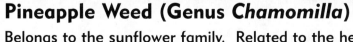

Pineapple Weed (Genus *Chamomilla*)

Belongs to the sunflower family. Related to the herb chamomile, which is used to make a relaxing tea

Habitat: trampled, grazed, or other disturbed places. Plants are less than 1 foot tall.

Flowers: what looks like a small pineapple is really a flowerhead densely packed with tiny tubelike flowers.

Fruit: hard seeds attached to stalks that look like inside-out umbrellas

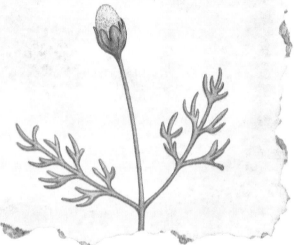

Besides collecting and identifying plants, Alice loved to write about them. She wrote articles about early collectors and traditional plant uses. She also wrote technical reports on how to tell different species of plants apart. In 1900, at the age of forty-one, Alice Eastwood wrote her second book—a guide to common flowers of the Rocky Mountains. And a year later, her flower guide for the Pacific Coast was published. These books made it easier for beginning flower watchers to identify their finds.

As Alice collected plants from up and down California, the academy's herbarium grew and grew. Alice also received plant specimens from herbariums all over the world in exchange for California plants. Alice was proud of the academy's collection and knew how important it was to other botanists. As scientists from around the world shared plant specimens, they were able to look for similarities between the plants and make discoveries about plant relationships.

Alice (on right) and some companions stop for a photograph on a botany trip in the Salmon and Trinity Mountains in California.

One April morning in 1906, Alice awoke to a rumble and roar—an earthquake! Unlike other earthquakes she had experienced, this one went on for a long time. Luckily, nothing was damaged in her room. But when she looked out from her home high up on Russian Hill, she saw plumes of smoke coming from the San Francisco waterfront. Quickly, Alice strode downhill through crowds of people escaping the fires and crumbling buildings. The earthquake had broken gas pipes in the city, and the leaking gas had started fires.

When Alice reached the academy, it looked undamaged. But a peek through the doorway revealed a pile of wreckage—and sky where there had once been a ceiling! She tried to get in, but the doorway was blocked. On the street, Alice ran into Robert Porter, one of her hiking partners, who offered to help her rescue the collections.

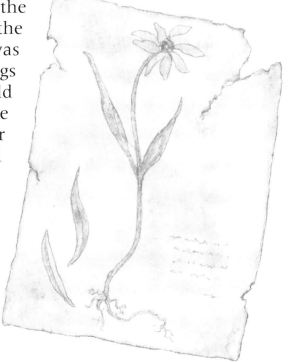

A custodian helped them get in the door, and inside, they found that the spiral marble staircase was shattered. Only the bronze railings and a few stairs were left. Could Alice and Robert make it up to the herbarium on the sixth floor without the stairs? Standing amid the rubble was the skeleton of a mastodon, an ancient elephant, on display. Alice calmly hung her lunch bag on its tusks, and then began to inch her way up the railings with Robert. They slowly made their way to the sixth floor like mountain climbers, trusting the railing to hold their weight.

In the herbarium, they discovered a complete mess. From smashed cases, Alice rescued as many plant specimens as she could and tied them into bundles. Luckily, she had saved bits of string from package wrappings over the years and had tied them into a large ball. Together, all these bits and pieces were long enough to reach from the sixth floor all the way to the ground level.

Alice carefully inched back down the railing to the bottom floor, and Robert lowered the bundles of plant specimens to her one by one. By this time, sparks from a burning factory next door were landing on the academy building. Alice and Robert had to get out before the whole museum went up in flames. Amid the chaos outside, they flagged down a wagon driver and loaded their scientific treasures into his wagon. Although they saved nearly 1,500 plant specimens, many others burned in the fire. Lost were Alice's collections from Colorado, Mount Tamalpais, and the northern coast of California. Many rare botany books and Alice's newly finished guide to trees also burned. Worst of all, the academy building was destroyed, and along with it, Alice's job went up in smoke.

Grove Karl Gilbert took this photograph of Alice by the fault line of the 1906 earthquake in California.

Fires continued to rage all over the city, and before they were under control, Russian Hill was also burning. Alice barely had time to pack a few of her own possessions in a small canvas bag before her own house was in flames. Suddenly, at the age of forty-seven, Alice was homeless and jobless. Among the possessions she saved were her typewriter, Bible, camera, family photograph album, best dress, and magnifying lens. She no longer had paying work, but she still had income from her rental houses in Colorado.

Alice was invited to stay with a family across the bay, in Berkeley. While there, she met Dr. Grove Karl Gilbert, a well-known **geologist** (a scientist who studies earth and rocks). Gilbert had explored vast areas of the West and was fascinated by the effects of the earthquake. He invited Alice to explore the earthquake fault with him. They saw a place where the quake had moved a garden twenty feet from its original location. Alice and Karl enjoyed each other's company, and this was the start of a long friendship.

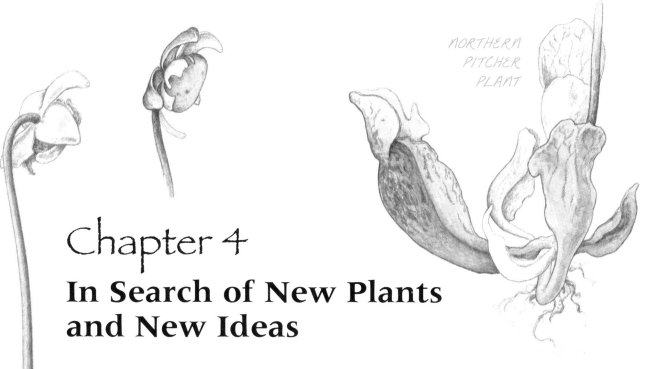

NORTHERN
PITCHER
PLANT

Chapter 4
In Search of New Plants and New Ideas

Alice stayed with her friends in Berkeley for a while, but in the fall of 1906, she visited her family in Denver and began to take advantage of her freedom. She didn't have much money, but she was so careful with what she had that she could afford to travel. For the next five years, Alice trekked the hills of California, the Rockies, and the swamps of the Deep South. She worked at the Gray Herbarium at Harvard University. She even journeyed across the Atlantic Ocean to England.

For a botanist, England was a treasure house. Alice visited all of the famous botanic gardens and herbaria that she could. Her special treat, however, was the opportunity to visit the famous botanist Sir Joseph Hooker, then ninety-four years of age. Hooker enthusiastically showed Alice his garden and the California plants growing there.

Ten months later, Alice sailed back to the United States. When she arrived in Boston, a letter from the California Academy of Sciences awaited her. They didn't have a new building yet, but they wanted her to come back and rebuild the herbarium collection. Alice moved to San Francisco once more. After six years, she could once again work for her own herbarium. But there was a lot to do. The herbarium had to be reorganized and more plants needed to be collected. During the next years of her life, Alice would venture off to Alaska and other faraway places to find plants.

What Is It?

Have you ever come across a flower that has several names? For example, one common plant called storksbill is also called clocks, fairy scissors, and filaree. Faced with this crazy system of multiple names, scientists tried giving one name to each plant, but the names ended up being very long. For example, one type of storksbill might have been called a red-stemmed, pink-flowered, hemlock-leaved bird's beak. What a mouthful!

Fortunately, in the 1700s, a young Swedish naturalist by the name of Carl Linnaeus invented a much simpler system for naming plants and animals. He devised names using a combination of words from the Greek and Latin languages. This system allowed scientists to create one name for each plant or animal without having to make it the length of a sentence. Linnaeus convinced others to use his system, and it continues to be used by scientists all over the world.

STORKSBILL

When Alice Eastwood began exploring the remote mountains, valleys, and forests of the West Coast, she spotted many plants that had not been named by scientists. For example, on Mount Tamalpais she had discovered several new species of the shrub called *Arctostaphylos* (*arco* means "bear," *staphylos* means "grape"). These elegant bushes have smooth red-brown stems, small thick leaves, and delicate bell-like flowers. All produce hard, red berries that resemble little apples. The Spanish called the plant *manzanita,* which means "little apple."

Alice noticed that the earliest blooming species of *Arctostaphylos* had gray leaves, so she called it *Arctostaphylos canescens* ("becoming gray"). Another species of manzanita had tiny glands on its hairy leaves that ooze a sticky substance. This one Alice named *Arctostaphylos glandulosa,* which means "full of glands." Alice named eleven of the sixty species of *Arctostaphylos* found in the world.

Alice Eastwood named hundreds of plants—and had many named after her. Various species of buckwheat, larkspur, sedge, lungwort, and many other plants bear her name. But the greatest honor of all was *Eastwoodia elegans* (elegant Eastwood). Alice had found this relative of the sunflower during her first collecting trip for the academy, and it was named after her by Townshend Brandegee.

Naming plants after collectors was one way to reward them for their work, since they often worked for little or no pay. Since people names don't tell much about a plant, descriptive names are now usually given to newly discovered plants.

Alice and Eastwoodia elegans, *a plant named after her*

Manzanita (genus *Arctostaphylos*)

In the heath family, which includes blueberries, huckleberries, and azaleas

Habitat: forests and brushy places from sea level to high mountains

Flower: pink or white bell-shaped blossoms with 10 stamens and 1 pistil

Fruit: dry berries with hard seeds. Can be eaten or mixed with water to make a cider

POINTLEAF MANZANITA

The Name Game

Inventing plant names is great practice for being a botanist. On your next visit to a flower patch, try making up your own descriptive names. Below are some things to consider as you ponder new names for neighborhood plants.

✔ Does the flower look like something? Does it resemble a dog, a fire engine, a tornado? Spacerockets and lady's slippers are examples of flowers named for what they look like.

✔ Can you use the colors or patterns you see to describe the plant? Where does it grow? Many plant names, such as marshmallow and meadowfoam, reflect the place where they are found.

Alice was fascinated by changes that she observed in **plant communities,** or groups of plants that live together. Over the years, she continued to tromp up and down the slopes of Mount Tamalpais. One of the most fascinating plant dramas she witnessed was the regrowth of plants after a fire. She wrote in a magazine article that the plants that rose from the ashes, such as manzanita and wild lilac, grew even more luxuriously than they had before the fire. After the first rains, some plants sprouted from undamaged roots, while others grew from seeds undamaged by fire. And some flowers that had been uncommon before the fire, such as golden eardrops, became more abundant. Another flower that commonly appears after fires has an appropriate name, fireweed.

Alice wrote that fire fertilized the soil, destroyed harmful bacteria, and cleared the ground for sun-loving plants. Fires scorched—but did not burn up—the seeds. Alice thought that perhaps the scorching was the signal for the seeds to sprout. The seeds must

NEW PLANT
GROWTH
FOLLOWING FIRE

have been resting under the dense shrubs for years until the right conditions came for them to grow once more.

Alice was one of the first botanists to write about the positive effects of natural fires, and it was many years before others were convinced of the importance of fire in wilderness areas. Eventually, managers of many parks and wild areas began to start fires on purpose to help restore the health of plant communities that rely on fire for clearing out old plant growth.

Fire isn't the only natural force that causes changes in plant communities. Floods, earthquakes, landslides, hurricanes, and erosion all bring changes to natural gardens. Animals such as burrowing gophers, rutting bucks, and gardening humans also have an impact. Whenever natural vegetation is disturbed and the ground is cleared, plant pioneers soon try to settle in. The pioneers that pop up in disturbed areas near human settlements are usually called weeds. Most weeds are simply plant pioneers that have journeyed with people, like stowaways, from one disturbed landscape to another. Others are native plants that grow best where land has been cleared or trampled. Like the plants Alice discovered after a fire, the seeds of these "weeds" wait in the soil until they get a chance to grow.

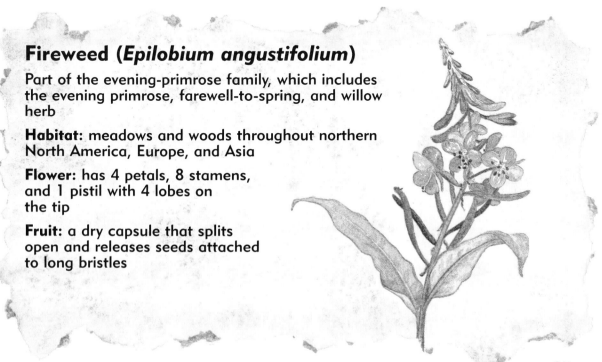

Fireweed (*Epilobium angustifolium*)

Part of the evening-primrose family, which includes the evening primrose, farewell-to-spring, and willow herb

Habitat: meadows and woods throughout northern North America, Europe, and Asia

Flower: has 4 petals, 8 stamens, and 1 pistil with 4 lobes on the tip

Fruit: a dry capsule that splits open and releases seeds attached to long bristles

Neighborhood Pioneers

To meet the plant pioneers in your neighborhood, try an experiment. This activity works best if you start it during spring or summer.

Supplies
✔ weed patch or part of a garden bed
✔ gardening tools
✔ tape measure or ruler
✔ 4 stakes (or sticks) 1 foot long
✔ 10 feet of twine or string
✔ journal and a pen or pencil
✔ flower field guide
✔ camera (optional)

Do Not Disturb Experiment in Progress

What to Do
Part One
✔ Get permission to clear a small plot of land (2 feet by 2 feet) in your yard, garden, school yard, or a vacant lot. Measure the plot and place a stake in each corner.

✔ Dig up the entire plot and remove every plant.

✔ With one end of the twine, tie a knot near the top of one stake. Wrap the twine around the top of each of the next three stakes, then tie another knot back at your first stake. You should have a roped-off square that looks like a boxing ring. You may also want to put up a sign that says, "Do Not Disturb. Experiment in Progress." (Put a clear plastic bag over your sign and tie it or tape it on to keep your sign dry.)

Part Two
✔ Keep an eye on the plot for the next few months. Check it often, and watch for plant pioneers. Once a week, count and write down the number of plants you find. If you have a camera, take photos once in a while. Be sure to record the date each picture was taken.

✔ As the plants mature and produce flowers, try to identify them. How many different kinds can you name? Make a list of what you find.

✔ If you can, watch the patch for a whole year or more and see what happens!

Though Alice was back to work at the academy, the temporary quarters were cramped, and it was hard to get any work done. When Alice got an offer to collect willows in the Far North, she jumped at the chance. In the spring of 1914, Alice traveled to the Yukon Territory, Canada, where she rented a miner's cabin in the village of Dawson. The cabin was far from cozy—the kitchen floor was covered with ice a foot thick. So Alice camped in the living room, where she kept a warm fire to dry her plant specimens and cook her food. During the spring and summer, she roamed the countryside, first collecting willow blooms and later their fruits. When Alice returned to San Francisco from the remote wilds of the Far North, she heard the terrible news that war had started in Europe. World War I had begun.

At age fifty-seven, Alice was getting settled once more. She had a home on Russian Hill with a view of San Francisco Bay and Mount Tamalpais. She had a cabin in Mill Valley, where she could spend nights during her weekend excursions and where she started a garden of rare and unusual plants from all over the world. She finally had a real herbarium in the brand-new academy buildings. And she had a proposal for marriage. Alice had been close to Grove Karl Gilbert for years, and now he wanted to marry her. A wedding was set for after his seventy-fifth birthday. Together they planned to care for his grandson, but tragically, Karl became ill and died May 1, 1918, five days before his birthday.

OGILVIE MOUNTAINS, YUKON TERRITORY

LITTLETREE WILLOW

Alice most likely sought solace again in work. She soon immersed herself in a new project. The new academy buildings were encircled by the peaceful woods and meadows of Golden Gate Park. For the previous thirty years, a determined Scotsman, John McClaren, had worked at transforming a windy landscape of shifting sand dunes on the edge of San Francisco into a large park. Wisely, he had set aside open space that could have otherwise become covered with concrete and houses.

BEACH PEA

Alice had known John McClaren for many years, and the two had shared the dream of creating a park filled with rare trees and shrubs from all over the world. The park could be a place for people to see the great diversity of the world's plants. To create such a garden, McClaren needed educated gardeners who knew about the uniqueness of each plant. Alice helped by teaching weekly botany classes for McClaren and his assistants. Grateful for this instruction, many of the gardeners helped Alice with the botanic garden at her cabin. There too they planted a variety of rare plants from around the world. The cabin soon became a gathering place for the gardening classes and Alice's large number of friends. But in July of 1929, a fire swept across the lower part of Mount Tamalpais. The cabin and garden went up in flames. Though many fire-tolerant plants survived, many plants were lost. Alice was so upset that she sold the property.

Meanwhile, Alice tried to start an arboretum, a place for the study of trees, in Golden Gate Park. Despite a lack of money for this project, Alice devised a plan to teach visitors about the park trees. With her own money, she bought a machine that could imprint plant names on aluminum cards. Each type of tree was labeled. Alice had hoped to print brochures and maps for visitors, but no money was available. Her dream would have to wait. Finally in 1938, a wealthy pioneer family left money to Golden Gate Park to create an arboretum. Alice's wish for a living tree museum had come true.

Green Museum

You too can start your own botanic garden by identifying and labeling neighborhood trees, shrubs, and wildflowers.

Supplies
✔ stiff paper
✔ colored markers
✔ stakes or sticks (bamboo shish kebab sticks work well)
✔ staples or thumbtacks
✔ plastic bags

What to Do
✔ Most plants in your neighborhood gardens won't be found in wildflower guides, but gardening books or neighborhood gardeners might help you identify them. A visit to a local plant nursery or botanic garden can also help.

✔ Before you start putting signs all over the place, ask the landowner (your folks or park staff, for example) for permission to label plants. Print the plant names on pieces of heavy paper and give each one a number. Cover each sign with a plastic bag to keep it dry.

✔ Attach each sign to a stake with staples or thumbtacks, then pound the stake into the ground next to the correct plant.

✔ Make a guide to teach garden visitors about your plants. Write down the name and number of each plant, then write anything interesting you may have learned about the plant. For example, you might tell where the plant originally comes from, if it has any special uses, or how it got its name. If it has an unusual aroma or texture, you might even suggest that people sniff or feel it.

If the plants you've labeled are spread all over your garden, you may want to make a map to help people locate each one. With a photocopier, you can make multiple copies of your guide so people can use it whenever they wish.

Chapter 5
Friend of Plants

Alice had always been healthy, but she was so busy with her work that she wore herself out. She spent her seventy-second birthday in the hospital, sick with pneumonia. Alice's sister, Kate, was living in San Francisco, and Alice moved into an apartment next door to her while she recovered. As Alice rested, she watched bulldozers preparing land for a new opera house. The area had once been a marsh where Alice had often searched for unusual plants. But like other wetlands, it was being drained to create more land for buildings.

San Francisco buzzed with activity. Wagons rumbled over cobbled streets. Motorcar drivers honked horns. Everywhere new houses were being built with lumber from the vast forests of the Pacific Coast. Like other cities, San Francisco was getting bigger, and so were the nearby towns. Every year, Alice watched as wild gardens were gobbled up by the spreading metropolis. On her journeys into the majestic forests of the rainy north country, she saw fewer forests and more stumps. She watched as towering redwoods were sliced into boards for building fancy Victorian homes.

Alice knew people needed homes, but she knew they also needed wild places like Mount Tamalpais for refuge from the bustle of city life. By the early 1900s, developers were already planning to build houses on the slopes of Mount Tamalpais. But Alice was not about to sit and watch this happen. As president of the Tamalpais

Conservation Club, she led a drive to collect money for land on Mount Tam before developers could buy it. With the assistance of the state of California and Congressman William Kent, most of Mount Tamalpais was made into a state park.

Over the years, Alice became involved in saving other wild areas. She wrote articles asking people to help save wildflowers by protecting them in parks and preserves. She helped form the Save-the-Redwoods League and participated in raising funds to buy the last remaining redwood forests before they were logged.

Shortly after her seventy-second birthday, Alice was hit by a car, and her left knee was badly crushed. She had to walk with a cane and found it hard to do her own collecting. So instead of exploring on horseback and foot, she traversed wild areas of the West in a used car. Driven by Tom Howell, the assistant curator of botany at the academy, her old car chugged over mountains and into dry desert washes. During expeditions, Tom and other friends collected plants, while Alice prepared the specimens for the academy's herbarium.

Assistant curator Tom Howell and Alice Eastwood traveled many miles in Lucy, a used car, looking for plants.

More than Ever

The fight to save wild places still goes on. In Northern California, most of the redwood forests have been cut down, and only a small number of ancient groves survive. Like Alice, you can help preserve ancient forests in California or wild places close to home. Ask your teacher for help or write to a local conservation club, native plant society, or a larger national conservation group, such as the Save-the-Redwoods League, 114 Sansome St., Room 605, San Francisco, CA 94104.

Alice continued to learn about plants from remote parts of the world, even when she was at home. Arctic explorer Louise Boyd brought Alice plants from Franz Josef Land. Ynes Mexia, a Mexican botanist, collected specimens for the herbarium from remote parts of Mexico and the vast rain forests of the Amazon.

Even in her eighties, Alice Eastwood didn't slow down. She was already an expert on the willow, manzanita, and Indian paintbrush, and at an age when most people were retired, she became an expert on a whole new group of flowers. Throughout the 1940s, she wrote a series of articles about the lupine, a type of pea flower. This didn't surprise her friends—they were used to watching Alice follow her passions.

Though Alice had only a high-school degree, she was highly respected by other scientists. They knew that her knowledge was based on years of careful investigation of plants. Several universities wanted to award Alice honorary college degrees, but she refused them. The natural rewards of years of plant study were honor enough for Alice!

During her last year of work at the herbarium, Alice wrote three articles on lilies, an article on junipers, and several reviews of other scientific articles. Then, at ninety years of age, she officially retired from the job as curator of botany at the California Academy of Sciences. But Alice did not stop working. Besides cataloging plants, she continued to seek out rare botany books for the herbarium library. This library had expanded along with the plant collection. Since the day Alice rescued nearly 1,500 herbarium specimens during the 1906 earthquake, the academy's plant collection had grown to more than 300,000!

This photo of Alice, hard at work, was taken just before her eightieth birthday.

Lupine (genus *Lupinus*)

Belongs to the pea family, which includes clover, locoweed, locust trees, and wild peas

Habitat: meadows, sand dunes, rocky hillsides, and even desert washes. Often abundant in poor soils or after a fire

Flowers: shaped like a butterfly. Usually blue and white

Fruit: a pea pod. Seeds are shot from the pod as it dries. The pea pods of some species can be poisonous.

In 1950, Alice was invited to Sweden for the Seventh International Botanical Congress. She had been to other gatherings of botanists from all over the world, but this time she would be the honorary president. Before her departure, a friend said, "How remarkable it is for a woman of your age to be starting on such a long flight alone!"

"Nothing remarkable about it all," Alice replied, "I've always flown!" Indeed, not only had Alice flown by airplane before, she had also flown on quick-stepping feet over mountain trails, and her eyes had traveled like fluttering butterflies over miles of flowers.

Now, at ninety-one, Alice traveled alone to Sweden, just as she had hiked alone in her younger years. She carried with her a hat decorated with daisies and another decorated with mushrooms. Reporters at the conference wrote articles about Alice that appeared in newspapers all over the world. They told tales of her adventurous explorations and important plant discoveries. They noted that she was the only woman who had been listed in every edition of American Men of Science. All this attention was exciting, but her biggest thrill was being invited to sit at the desk where Carl Linnaeus had written about botany two hundred years before.

Two years later, Alice was honored during the one hundredth anniversary of the California Academy of Sciences. The announcement was made that the academy planned to build a new museum wing called the Alice Eastwood Hall of Botany. This was to be Alice's last visit to the herbarium. She had spent over seventy-five years studying flowers. Whether she was examining dried flowers in the herbarium or discovering a new flower outdoors, Alice was continually amazed and thrilled by them. Tom Howell said that she was always willing to teach anyone who loved flowers as she did.

In October 1953, Alice died at the age of ninety-four. The next spring, a redwood preserve in Northern California was set aside in her honor. You can visit the immense trees in the Alice Eastwood Grove, not far from Redwood National Park. They stand tall and carry on the memory of the naturalist who protected them.

Alice's life had been like a lush flower garden. The raspberry blossoms in her uncle's garden, the arctic willows she collected in the Yukon, the manzanita of Mount Tamalpais—all these and more bloomed inside Alice's fertile mind. Keep exploring flower fields, and poppies may pop out of your ears. Buttercups may shine from your eyes. You, like Alice Eastwood, can have a life bursting with wild beauty and adventures.

Alice Eastwood, at ninety-one years old, proudly seated in Carl Linnaeus's chair in Sweden

Important Dates

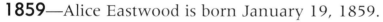

WESTERN TAILED
BLUE BUTTERFLY

1859—Alice Eastwood is born January 19, 1859.

1865—Mother dies

1867—Moves to convent

1873—Joins father in Denver, Colorado

1879—Graduates from high school, begins teaching

1887—Guides Alfred Russel Wallace up Grays Peak

1890—Quits teaching to become a full-time botanist

1892—Begins working at California Academy of Sciences in San Francisco

1901—Key and Flora, Pacific Coast Edition published

1906—San Francisco earthquake destroys Academy of Sciences building. Alice Eastwood one of few women listed in American Men of Science

1911—Visits England

1912—Returns to her job as curator at the California Academy of Sciences

1914—Explores in Alaska and the Yukon Territory

1916—New California Academy of Sciences building opens to the public.

1918—Grove Karl Gilbert dies.

1926—Helps start the San Francisco Garden Club

1928—Elected fellow, or honored member, of the California Academy of Sciences

1938—Golden Gate Park receives funds for an arboretum.

1949—Retires as curator. Camp Alice Eastwood, a group campground, dedicated in Mount Tamalpais State Park

1950—Honorary president of the Seventh International Botanical Congress

1953—Dies October 30

Answers for page 20:
1. rough-fruited cinquefoil, 2. bulbous buttercup, 3. evening primrose, 4. field mustard

Glossary

botanists: people who study plants

geologist: a person who studies rocks and land forms

herbarium: (plural, herbaria) a museum of dried and pressed plants

mesas: flat-topped mountains or ridges

naturalists: people who study nature

nectar: the sweet substance produced by flowers that is often food for insects

petals: the colored, leaflike parts of a flower

pistil: the female part of a flower

plant communities: groups of plants living together

pollen: a capsule that contains a plant's male sex cells

sepals: leaflike structures attached at the base of a flower

species: a group of plants or animals with common traits

stamens: the male parts of a flower, which contain pollen

BLEEDING HEART

RUBY-THROATED
HUMMINGBIRD

Alice Eastwood was a lifelong lover of flowers.

Bibliography

Bonta, Marcia Myers. "Alice Eastwood, Grand Old Botanist of the Academy." *Women in the Field: America's Pioneering Women Naturalists.* College Station, Tex.: Texas A&M University Press, 1991.

Dakin, Susanna Bryant. *Perennial Adventure: A Tribute to Alice Eastwood.* San Francisco: California Academy of Sciences, 1954.

Eastwood, Alice. *Key and Flora, Pacific Coast Edition.* Boston: Ginn and Company, 1901.

———. "California Herb Lore—*Rhamnus californicus.*" *Erythea,* 5:98 (September 1897).

———. "Plant Inhabitants of Nob Hill, San Francisco." *Erythea,* 6:61-67 (June 1898).

———. Papers. San Francisco: California Academy of Sciences.

Wilson, Carol Green. *Alice Eastwood's Wonderland: The Adventures of a Botanist.* San Francisco, Calif. California Academy of Sciences, 1955.

Quotations from *Alice Eastwood's Wonderland: The Adventures of a Botanist* by Carol Wilson Green used with permission from the California Academy of Sciences.

Index

All photographs are reproduced through the courtesy of Special Collections, California Academy of Sciences, except p. 30, G.K. Gilbert/United States Geological Survey and p. 44, © Dagens Bild.

HAY LIBRARY
WESTERN WYOMING COMMUNITY COLLEGE